CHANGING COURSE GRACEFULLY:

A Strategic Guide to Building Foundational Self-Trust

ELAINA KELLY SMITH

VENTURES
& BLOOM
PRESS

Changing Course Gracefully: A Strategic Guide to Building Foundational Self-Trust

Published by Ventures & Bloom Press 221 W 10th Street #48, Wilmington, DE 19801 connect@ventureandbloompress.com www.ventureandbloompress.com

Important Disclaimers:

The information in this book is for educational purposes only and is not intended to replace professional medical, psychological, or financial advice. The author, Elaina Kelly Smith, is not a licensed medical or mental healthcare provider. This book is not intended to be used to diagnose, treat, or cure any condition. Consult qualified professionals for specific health concerns.

The author's story and experiences are her own. The PARQS™ Method is a "practical framework" for personal navigation, not a therapeutic prescription.

The breathing techniques and mindfulness practices presented, such as "Box Breathing" and the "grounding exercise using your five senses", are generally safe for most people. However, discontinue any practice that causes discomfort. If you have respiratory conditions, anxiety disorders, or other health concerns, consult your healthcare provider before beginning these practices.

First Edition

Printed in the United States of America

Publisher's Cataloging-in-Publication Data
Names: Smith, Elaina Kelly, author.
Title: Changing course gracefully: a strategic guide to building foundational self-trust / Elaina Kelly Smith.
Description: Includes bibliographical references and index. | Wilmington, DE: Ventures & Bloom Press, 2025.

Identifiers: LCCN: 2025923803 | ISBN: 979-8-9936727-6-2 (paperback) | 979-8-9936727-7-9 (eBook)

Subjects: LCSH Self-actualization (Psychology) | Self-trust. | Mindfulness (Psychology) | Decision-making. | Imposter phenomenon. | Self-help. | BISAC SELF-HELP / Personal Growth / General | SELF-HELP / Self-Management / General

Classification: LCC BF637.S4 S65 2025 | DDC 158--dc23

For my brothers, Adrian (always in my heart) and Anthony, whose unconditional love, steady support, and devotion to their own families have always shown me the way.

And for Sydney and Joseph, whose unwavering belief in me taught me how to find my own way.

Table of Contents

Part 4: The PARQS Field Guide:
Navigating Complex Terrain

A Personal Note: My Journey

I know the feeling of being on autopilot intimately. For years, my own life was an odyssey out of that exact state. On paper, everything looked fine—I had built successful businesses and had the freedom to pursue my interests. But inside, I felt a persistent sense of emptiness and a lack of satisfaction with my accomplishments.

Because I was emotionally dissociated from myself, I would chronically agree to things, guided by a relentless chorus of "shoulds" rather than my own inner voice. I didn't have a framework to bring this "Remote Control Living" to the front so I could see it for what it was. The turning point wasn't a dramatic epiphany, but a simple, quiet question from my therapist. In the middle of a session, she paused and asked me, "What does Elaina want?"

That question started the "brick by brick" process of putting the pieces together. It was the first step in realizing that I had been living a life that was not truly my own. The PARQS™ Framework is not a theory I read in a book; it is the toolkit I built for myself during that odyssey. It is composed of the real, practical strategies I used to find my way back to a life of clarity, purpose, and self-chosen action. I share it with you as a fellow traveler who knows the territory of being lost and, more importantly, has found a way home.

How to Use This Book:
A Note on the Practices

The exercises, reflections, and tools in the coming chapters are invitations, not prescriptions.

You are the ultimate authority on your own body, your history, and your well-being. As you move through this framework, please remember:

- **Trust Your Timing:** Some practices may resonate deeply right away, while others may not feel right for you at this moment. That is perfectly okay.
- **Trust Your "No":** The goal of this work is to deepen your self-trust. That begins with trusting your own responses to this material. If a practice feels overwhelming or incorrect for you, you have full permission to skip it or adapt it.
- **Take What Connects:** Take what connects with you now, and leave what doesn't connect—yet.

This book is a map, but you are the navigator.

PART 1

The PARQS Framework

Chapter 1:
Introduction to The PARQS™ Framework

You know the feeling. It's a quiet, persistent hum in the background of a life that—by every external standard—looks perfect.

On paper, the checklist is complete. You have the career, the stability, and the responsibilities of a capable adult. You are the person others rely on to fix, to serve, and to support. You show up, you deliver, and you keep the machinery of your life running smoothly.

But on the inside, there is a nagging disconnection—a sense of being a passenger in your own vehicle.

I call this **"Remote Control Living."**

It is the state of moving through your days on autopilot, guided not by your own internal signal, but by a relentless chorus of "shoulds" and expectations. It's the feeling that the channel is being changed by someone else—by your family, your culture, your job, or by the momentum of the past choices you made before you knew better.

You can spot Remote Control Living by the specific type of exhaustion it creates. You aren't just tired from a long day of work; you are tired from the **friction**. It is the friction of moving through the world in a way that isn't truly your own, wearing a costume that doesn't quite fit, day after day.

The most unnerving symptom of this state usually happens in the quiet moments. It happens when the noise stops, the demands pause, and someone—a friend, a therapist, or just your own reflection—asks you a question:

"What do you want?"

For many of us, the silence that follows is deafening.

We have spent so long tuning into the frequencies of others that we have lost the signal to our own preferences. We look inward and find a blank space where our desires should be.

If you recognize yourself in this description, I want you to take a breath. **This is not a personal failure.** You are not broken. You are navigating with an uncalibrated compass.

We all have the capacity for internal guidance. But like any skill, when it goes unused, it gets rusty. Through the noise of external expectations and the weight of self-criticism, we lose our bearings. We begin to second-guess our intuition, defer our decisions, and look outside ourselves for permission to exist.

This book is how we get the controller back.

This is not a book of "magic cures" or spiritual bypasses. It is a practical, down-to-earth toolkit. It is a guide to reconnecting with the decision-making tools you already possess but have forgotten how to use.

We are going to rebuild your foundation of self-trust, brick by brick.

The PARQS™ Framework is a set of five interconnected practices designed to interrupt the signal of Remote Control Living and restore your own voice. These are not abstract theories; they are tangible skills for navigating your actual life.

They are:

- **Preferences (Self-Honesty):** The skill of identifying what you *actually* want, separate from the noise of "should."
- **Awareness (Self-Regulation):** The skill of using your body's physical feedback to understand where you are right now.
- **Right Action (Self-Integrity):** The skill of matching your actions to your truth, building momentum through purposeful movement.
- **Questions (Self-Compassion):** The skill of interrupting the Inner Critic to re-orient yourself when you get lost.
- **Self-Acceptance (Self-Loyalty):** The skill of committing to be on your own side, no matter what.

Underpinning all of these is **Radical Self-Responsibility**: the commitment to take ownership of this journey. I can give you the map, but you are the navigator.

A Moment to Check In

Reflect on your day. Think about your day so far. Can you identify one small moment—no matter how brief—where you felt like you were on "autopilot"?

Notice the signs. Maybe it was saying "yes" to an invitation you dreaded. Maybe it was scrolling through your phone to numb out a feeling of anxiety.

Acknowledge it. Do not judge it. Do not try to fix it yet. The first step in taking back the remote control is admitting that, for a moment, you weren't the one holding it.

Let's begin.

Reflections

Chapter 2:
Preferences (The P in PARQS)

In the introduction, we established that Remote Control Living is a navigational problem. You are adrift without a clear sense of direction.

The first practice of The PARQS™ Framework solves this problem directly. It establishes your "True North."

To navigate, you must be able to answer the most fundamental question of the itinerary: **"What do I actually want?"**

This is the practice of **Preferences**.

For many of us, this question is excruciating to answer. We have spent decades making decisions based on what we *should* want, what others expect of us, or what seems like the responsible choice. The voice of our authentic preference has been drowned out by the noise of obligation.

We treat our own desires as optional, while treating the expectations of others as mandatory.

This is not a character flaw; it is a mechanical failure. Your "Preference Muscle" has simply grown weak from lack of use.

Rebuilding it is the starting point for self-trust.

Identifying Is Not Acting

We often avoid asking "What do I want?" because we are afraid of the answer. We worry that if we acknowledge a desire—to leave a job, to rest, to say no—we are obligated to act on it immediately, consequences be damned.

Let's be clear: **Identifying a Preference is not the same as acting on it.**

This practice is about **Self-Honesty**. It is the act of acknowledging your own reality. Without this information, you are navigating blind. You cannot make an informed decision if you are withholding half the truth from yourself.

Why It's Hard to Answer

This was the pivot point in my own journey.

For years, I sat in my therapist's office, and when she asked, "What does Elaina want?", I went blank.

It wasn't that I was being difficult. I genuinely could not find the signal. I had spent so long serving, fixing, and supporting that I had lost the ability to access my own needs.

I realized I couldn't think my way to the answer. I had to rehabilitate the muscle. I started not with grand life changes, but with a specific tool.

Pausing to Ask "Actually...?"

The primary tool for this practice is designed to create a pocket of space between a request and your response. In that space, you check in.

Here is how it works:

The next time you are asked to do something—whether it's a colleague asking for help or a family member inviting you to dinner—do not give your automatic "yes."

Stop. Take one breath. Ask yourself:

"Actually, what do I want right now?"

You do not have to say "no." You do not have to explain yourself. You do not even have to change your answer.

The goal of this step is to **notice**. You are gathering information.

Every time you perform this pause, you interrupt the autopilot. You teach your nervous system that your voice is a factor in the decision-making process.

What If My Mind Goes Blank?

When you first try this, you may hear nothing.

This silence is your confirmation that the autopilot has been in charge for a long time. In these moments, do not force an answer. Ask a different question.

Instead of "What do I want?", ask:

"What am I actively trying to avoid right now?"

Sometimes, it is easier to identify what hurts than what heals. Recognizing that you *don't* want to do something is a valid preference. It counts.

When You Can't Get What You Want

The most common objection I hear is this: *"What if I know my preference, but my responsibilities make it impossible?"*

Example: Your boss asks you to stay late. Your Preference is to go home. You need the job.

If you ignore your Preference and stay late on autopilot, you will build resentment. You will feel like a victim of your circumstances.

Use the compass:

1. **Pause.** Ask "Actually, what do I want?"

2. **Acknowledge the truth:** "I want to go home."

3. **Make a conscious choice:** "I am choosing to stay late because I value my security."

The outcome is the same—you stay late—but the internal experience is entirely different. You are no longer a victim; you are a navigator making a hard choice. You have validated your own reality.

A Moment to Check In

Catch the impulse. The next time you are about to say "yes" to a request—whether from a colleague or a family member, perform the pause.

Ask the question. Before the word leaves your mouth, take one breath. Ask yourself: *"Do I actually want to do this, or do I feel like I should?"*

Observe the data. Notice your internal response. You do not have to change your answer or your action yet. Your only task is to notice. That answer is your True North.

Reflections

Chapter 3:
Awareness (The A in PARQS)

If the practice of Preferences is about identifying your destination, the practice of Awareness is about figuring out where you are on the map right now. It is the second essential skill in The PARQS™ Framework. This is where we stop looking outside for information and start listening to the feedback provided by our own bodies.

For many of us who are used to thinking our way through problems, this can feel counterintuitive. We trust our intellect above all else. But when you're stuck in "Remote Control Living," your mind is often the most unreliable narrator, conditioned by years of "shoulds" and external expectations. It will rationalize, justify, and talk you into choices that feel logical but leave you feeling empty.

Your body, however, doesn't know how to lie.

I have found that the body is one of the most honest feedback loops we have. It is always in the now, constantly sending signals about your emotional state through physical sensations—a tight jaw, a fluttering in your stomach, a sense of warmth in your chest.

For me, the most powerful teacher of Awareness wasn't a quiet meditation hall; it was the sensory overload of a busy street in Siem Reap, Cambodia. The city planning was completely different from what I was used to. In a single glance, I could see someone burning trash, a fruit cart serving customers, and oxen walking down the road. My brain was trying to process a dozen conflicting signals at once, and I could feel my shoulders creeping up towards my ears. In that moment of overwhelm, I had a choice: I could either get lost in the feeling or use it as a cue to practice.

Grounding with Your Five Senses

This is a tool for pulling yourself out of the noise of your mind and anchoring you in your physical surroundings. It takes less than a minute, and you can use it anywhere—in a boardroom, on a plane, or at your kitchen counter.

What it is: An exercise where you methodically name things you can perceive with your five senses. **What it does:** It interrupts the cycle of anxious thoughts and brings your focus back to the present moment, calming your nervous system.

Here's how to do it:

1. Name **5** things you can see around you.
2. Name **4** things you can feel.
3. Name **3** things you can hear.
4. Name **2** things you can smell.
5. Name **1** thing you can taste.

That's it. In that moment in Cambodia, instead of just enduring the discomfort, I consciously chose to use this tool. I focused on the color of a piece of fruit, the feeling of my feet in my shoes, the sound of a distant motorbike. By the time I was done, the tension in my shoulders had eased. I hadn't changed the street, but I had changed my experience of it.

This is the practice of Awareness. It's not about waiting for a "gut feeling." It is the gentle, "brick by brick" process of re-establishing the connection to your body and trusting that whatever you find—whether it's a knot in your stomach or a quiet sense of nothing at all—is valid information.

A Moment to Check In

Scan your body. Right now, take a moment to notice your physical self. Where do you hold tension first? Your neck? Your stomach? Your jaw?

Label the signal. That sensation is your built-in alarm system. It is your personal cue to practice Awareness.

Reflections

Chapter 4:
Right Action (The R in PARQS)

So far in The PARQS™ Framework, we have learned how to identify our destination with Preferences and how to read our current location with Awareness. But a map and a compass are only useful if you are willing to move. Insight without action is just information. It's the practice of Right Action that turns self-awareness into self-trust.

This is the third and most tangible skill in the framework. It's the practice of Self-Integrity—the conscious choice to match your external actions with your internal truth. Every time you take a small step that honors your authentic preference, you send a powerful message to yourself: "I am on my own side. I trust what I know."

This is where many of us get stuck. We wait for a "big aha moment" or a bolt of lightning to propel us into a new life. We believe that meaningful change has to be dramatic, disruptive, and perfectly executed. But that belief is a trap. It keeps us paralyzed, waiting for a perfect moment that never comes. The 'brick by brick' philosophy is most critical here. Self-trust is not built by making a giant leap across a canyon. It is built by laying one brick, taking one small step that matches your direction.

Right Action vs. Perfect Action

The greatest obstacle to taking Right Action is the myth of "perfect" action. We often wait until we have the perfect words, the perfect timing, or a guarantee of a perfect outcome before we act. This waiting is a form of paralysis. Right Action is not about perfection. It is about courage. It is about taking the next small, messy, courageous step in the direction that feels most aligned with your integrity, even when you are uncertain of the outcome.

One of the most powerful Right Actions you can learn is how to change your mind. Autopilot programming can make us feel that once we have said "yes" to something, we are locked in. To change course would be rude, flaky, or difficult. But Self-Loyalty requires that we give ourselves permission to make a new choice when we receive new information—even if that new information is simply a clearer understanding of our own needs.

While in Malaysia, my tour guide invited me to visit a 100-year-old market. Intrigued, my automatic response was "yes". But as we drove, my Awareness kicked in. I noticed a growing tension in my body. The excitement I thought I "should" feel simply wasn't there. What was present was a deep sense of fatigue. My Preference was not for a bustling market; it was for rest.

In that moment, I realized my automatic "yes" was a betrayal of my own needs. The only way to act on my preference was to take a Right Action, even if it felt uncomfortable. I leaned forward and said, politely and clearly, "I've realized I'm more tired than I thought. Please take me back to my hotel."

Was it a little awkward? Yes. But the feeling of relief that washed over me was immediate and deep. That small, uncomfortable act of self-integrity was a powerful deposit in my self-trust account.

It was evidence that I would stand by myself, even when it was inconvenient.

A Moment to Check:

Shrink the goal. Bring to mind one goal or desire that feels heavy right now.

Find the micro-step. Ask yourself: *"What is the smallest possible action I can take in that direction today?"* It might be sending one email, doing one push-up, or saving one dollar.

Take the action. Identify it. Do it. That is a Right Action.

Reflections

Chapter 5:
Questions (The Q in PARQS)

The journey out of "Remote Control Living" is not a straight line. There will be days when you forget to pause and ask, *'**actually**, what do I want?'*, when you ignore the signals from your body, or when a Right Action feels impossible. In those moments, it is not your willpower that fails you; it is the quality of your questions.

For most of us, the internal monologue is dominated by questions that are disguised accusations: *'What is wrong with me?' 'Why can't I get this right?'*

These are not genuine inquiries; they are dead ends. They do not produce answers; they produce shame. They are the voice of the Inner Critic, and their only function is to keep you stuck.

The fourth practice in The PARQS™ Framework is about learning to ask better Questions. This is the skill of Self-Compassion in action. It is the tool you use to interrupt the downward spiral of self-criticism and re-orient yourself toward a more productive path.

The Power of
a Compassionate Question

A compassionate question does not assume a negative answer. It opens up a space for curiosity, learning, and growth. It shifts you from being the defendant in your own courtroom to being a curious explorer of your own experience. These questions often start with "What" or "How":

- *"What can I learn from this?"*
- *"What support do I need right now?"*
- *"How can I approach this differently next time?"*

This shift is subtle, but its impact is significant. One type of question leads to a dead end of shame; the other opens up a path forward.

For years, my inner dialogue after making a mistake was a harsh cross-examination. My work was to consciously practice replacing that with a single, compassionate question. Instead of asking, *"Why did you do that?"* I learned to ask, *"Okay, what did you learn?"* As my practice deepened, I added a question that challenged me even more: How can I benefit from this moment?

This is not about pretending a difficult situation is 'good.' It is about utility. It is the practice of Radical Self-Responsibility: refusing to leave a painful moment empty-handed. You are mining the experience for value you can use moving forward.

Each of these small shifts was another brick laid in the foundation of my self-trust. It helped me transform moments of confusion into useful information for my growth.

A Moment to Check In

Audit your Inner Critic. What is your Inner Critic's favorite judgmental question? (e.g., *"Why are you so lazy?"* or *"What is wrong with you?"*).

Flip the script. Write that question down. Now, consciously rephrase it into a compassionate question that starts with **"What"** or **"How."** *(e.g., "What support do I need right now?" or "How can I make this easier?")*

Reflections

Chapter 6:
Self-Acceptance (The S in PARQS)

We have arrived at the final practice of The PARQS™ Framework, and it is the one that holds all the others together. It is the practice of Self-Acceptance. For many of us, the word "acceptance" can be challenging. It can sound like resignation, like giving up. We are wired to fix, to improve, to strive. But in this framework, Self-Acceptance is not about passivity. It is the most active and courageous practice of all. It is the practice of Self-Loyalty.

Self-Loyalty is the unwavering commitment to be on your own side, no matter what. It's the practice of treating yourself with the same kindness and understanding you would offer a dear friend who has stumbled. It is the antidote to the perfectionism that keeps so many of us stuck. The journey of building self-trust is, by its very nature, messy. There will be "re-dos." This is not a sign of failure. It is a sign that you are human. Self-Acceptance is the skill you use in those moments. It's what allows you to pick yourself up, consult your internal guidance system again, and move forward without judgment.

Permission for Physical Release

Before we can mentally accept a difficult situation, we often need to acknowledge the physical reality of our emotions. Feelings like frustration, anger, or disappointment are not just thoughts; they are energy in the body. Trying to "think" your way out of that energy without first allowing it to move is like trying to calm a shaking bottle by telling it to be still. The first step in genuine self-acceptance is often giving yourself permission for a safe, physical release. This doesn't have to be dramatic. It might mean:

- Finding a private space to stomp your feet.
- Exhaling with a loud, deep sigh.
- Pressing your palms firmly against a wall for a few seconds.

By discharging the physical energy, you create the space for your mind to follow.

PRACTICAL TOOL:

The "Of Course" Statement

Once you have allowed for that physical release, you can offer yourself one of the most powerful tools in the PARQS toolkit: the "Of course" Statement. This is a phrase that validates your experience instantly.

How to Use It:

When the wave of emotion hits, say it out loud:

- *"Of course I am overwhelmed; I have never done this before."*
- *"Of course I am angry; my boundary was just crossed."*
- *"Of course I am tired; I have been running on adrenaline for weeks."*

Be specific. The more specific you are, the more your nervous system will relax.

As my own practice deepened, I realized that "Of Course" was more than just a phrase. It became my internal cheer team, a powerful declaration of Self-Loyalty. I discovered that within these two words was an entire framework for how to stand by myself.

Why This Works: The Logic of Emotion

When we feel overwhelmed, our Inner Critic usually attacks us with "Why?" (*Why are you so sensitive? Why can't you handle this?*). This sends the nervous system into a defense spiral.

The phrase **"Of course"** is the antidote because it creates instant **validation**.

It signals to your brain that your reaction makes sense given your history, current stress level, and the situation at hand. It creates a pause where you stop fighting reality and start working *with* it. You are telling yourself: *I make sense. My feelings have a cause. I am safe to feel this.*

A Moment to Check In

Bring a mistake to mind. Think of a mistake you made recently. Notice how your Inner Critic speaks to you about it.

Validate the reason. Now, try the **Of Course** tool. Fill in the blank: *"Of course I made that mistake, because..."* (e.g., I was rushing, I was tired, I didn't have all the info).

Feel the loyalty. Notice what shifts in your body when you validate the reason instead of attacking the result. That settling feeling is Self-Loyalty.

Reflections

Chapter 7:
Putting It All Together

We have spent the last five chapters exploring the individual practices of The PARQS™ Framework. We've learned to identify our Preferences, to listen to our body's Awareness, to take Right Action, to ask better Questions, and to practice Self-Acceptance. Each of these is a powerful tool on its own. But their true power is unlocked when you learn to use them together, not as a rigid, step-by-step checklist, but as a fluid and interconnected system.

This chapter is where we move from learning the notes to playing the music.

Your Compass Is a Multi-Tool, Not a Checklist

PARQS is not a linear recipe. Life is rarely that neat.

Think of your compass less as a checklist and more as a **multi-tool**. You do not unfold every blade and screwdriver at once. You assess the situation and select the one tool you need most in that moment.

Any element can be your entry point.

I had a direct experience of this at an airport when my departure gate was changed three times in under an hour, sending a rush of passengers hurrying across the terminal. My immediate reaction was a jolt of stress. I was on autopilot, caught up in the collective anxiety. Then, my practice kicked in.

- **Entry Point: Awareness.** I consciously noticed the tension in my shoulders and the shallow rhythm of my breath. I caught the story my mind was broadcasting: *You are going to miss this flight!*
- **Pivot to Right Action.** My first Right Action was to stop. I stood still in the middle of the corridor and took two deep breaths. This small physical pause interrupted the panic loop.
- **Engage Questions.** Now that my brain was back online, I asked: *"What are my options here, besides running?*
- **Another Right Action.** I looked around and spotted an airport attendant driving an electric cart. The next Right Action was to walk over and ask for a ride to the new gate.
- **The Result: Self-Acceptance.** I arrived at the gate with time to spare, feeling calm and centered. In that moment, I practiced Self-Acceptance by acknowledging that I had navigated a stressful situation with intention.

In this one small event, I fluidly used four of the five elements, not in order, but as the situation demanded. This is the PARQS compass in action. The practices feed and inform one another, creating a continuous loop of self-discovery and self-trust.

A Moment to Check In

Identify the challenge. Think about a small, recurring challenge in your life—perhaps a conversation you have been avoiding or a task you keep procrastinating on.

Select your tool. Do not try to solve the whole problem. Ask yourself: **Which of the five PARQS tools does this situation demand right now?**

- Do you need honesty? (Preference)
- Do you need to calm down? (Awareness)
- Do you need to move? (Right Action)
- Do you need a new perspective? (Questions)
- Do you need to stop beating yourself up? (Self-Acceptance)

Trust your reach. Noticing which tool, you instinctively reach for is the first step in putting it all together.

Reflections

Chapter 8:
Living with Empowered Self-Trust

We began this book with the "unnamed feeling"—that quiet, persistent sense of being a passenger in your own life. We called it "Remote Control Living," a state of disconnection from your own inner guidance system. The journey through The PARQS™ Framework has been a "brick by brick" process of rebuilding that connection and constructing a foundation of self-trust.

This final chapter is not about learning a new skill. It is about what comes next. It's about taking the compass you have recalibrated and using it to navigate the rest of your life. This is where we transition from building self-trust to living with empowered self-trust.

There is no finish line. There is no perfect, final state of "arrival." Life will continue to present challenges, detours, and moments of uncertainty. The difference is that you are no longer navigating blind. You now have a set of reliable, practical tools you can return to, again and again. You have a process for listening to yourself, for taking matched action, for course-correcting with compassion, and for remaining loyal to your own journey.

Living with empowered self-trust means the PARQS practices shift from a conscious checklist to an intuitive reflex.

At first, you have to stop and manually reach for the compass. But over time, the pause becomes automatic. The question *'What do I actually want?'* arises before the autopilot can take over.

This is not about being bulletproof. It is about Self-Reliability. It is the bone-deep knowledge that no matter what life throws at you, you have a system to handle it. You are on your own side.

A Moment to Check In

Look back. Take a moment to reflect on the person who started Chapter 1. Now, look at where you are today.

Find the evidence. Identify one piece of evidence that you are different. Is your Inner Critic less aggressive? Did you pause before saying "yes" this week?

Acknowledge the shift. That change is not an accident. That is the feeling of your own foundation, built brick by brick.

Reflections

PART 2

PARQS in Action:
A Practical Guide Chapter

Chapter 9:
PARQS for Everyday Decisions

You have seen how the PARQS compass can guide you through a high-stress moment. Now, we bring it into the place where the real work of building self-trust is done: the small, everyday choices that make up your life.

The journey out of "Remote Control Living" is not defined by a few dramatic, life-altering decisions. It is forged in the cumulative effect of hundreds of small, conscious choices—the choices that make up your day, which in turn make up your week, your year, and ultimately, your life. It is in the quiet moments—deciding what to eat, how to spend a Saturday, or when to close your laptop—that you build the muscle of self-trust.

These are not throwaway moments. They are your training ground.

If you habitually override your preference in the small things, you teach your nervous system that your needs are negotiable. When the big decisions arrive, you will not have the evidence file to back yourself up. We start small so we can stand tall later.

The "What's for Dinner?" Decision

This is a choice so common that it's almost invisible, which makes it the perfect training ground.

- **Autopilot:** You open the fridge, feel overwhelmed, and order the same takeout you always do, not because you want it, but because it's easy.
- **PARQS in Action:**
  - » **(P)reference:** You pause and ask, *"What does my body actually want to eat right now?"* Maybe it's something light and fresh, or something warm and comforting.
  - » **(A)wareness:** You notice you're feeling tired and don't have the energy for a complex meal.
  - » **(Q)uestion:** You ask, *"How can I respect my preference for a fresh meal and my need for something easy?"*
  - » **(R)ight Action:** You decide to pick up a pre-made salad from the grocery store instead of cooking.
  - » **(S)elf-Acceptance:** You enjoy your meal, feeling good about the fact that you made a choice that respected both your desires and your reality.

This entire process might take 60 seconds, but the impact is profound. You have just sent yourself a clear message: "My needs matter, even in the small things."

SCENARIO 2:

The "Saturday Shoulds" Decision

It is Saturday morning. Your body feels heavy with the fatigue of the week, but your mind presents a long list of "shoulds": *clean the house, run errands, catch up on email.*

- **Autopilot Response:** You push through. You treat your body like a machine that needs to be driven. By 8:00 p.m., you collapse—not satisfied, but resentful. You "won" the to-do list but lost your weekend.
- **PARQS in Action:**
  - » **(P)reference:** You acknowledge the data: *I need rest.*
  - » **(A)wareness:** You notice the anxiety rising when you think about *not* being productive.
  - » **(R)ight Action:** You negotiate. You do one high-priority errand to satisfy the need for order, then give yourself full permission to do nothing for three hours.
  - » **(S)elf-Acceptance:** When the guilt creates a ping of "I should be doing more," you meet it with **Of Course**: *"Of course I feel lazy; I am addicted to productivity. Today, I am choosing to rest."*

You end the day feeling restored, not drained. You have acted with integrity, building more evidence that you can trust yourself to take care of yourself.

A Moment to Check In

Name the drain. Name one recurring decision that drains you. (e.g., The morning commute, the "what's for dinner" debate, or the Sunday night schedule review).

Run the experiment. Next time you face this moment, **stop.** Do not let the habit make the choice for you. Apply **one** element of the compass (like pausing to ask *"Actually...?"* or taking one conscious breath).

Observe the result. Interrupt the pattern once. Then, observe. Do not look for fireworks. You might feel a shift, or you might feel awkward. **Both are valid.** The victory is that **you showed up for yourself** in a moment where you usually disappear.

Reflections

Chapter 10:
PARQS for Difficult Conversations

We have applied our PARQS compass to the external chaos of the world and the internal landscape of our own choices. Now, we bring it to the place where those two worlds meet with the greatest force: our relationships with others. Difficult conversations are a fact of life. Asking for a raise, setting a boundary with a family member, or disagreeing with a partner—these moments are often where our "autopilot" programming is strongest. We might fall into old patterns of people-pleasing, shutting down, or becoming defensive. These reactions are driven by fear—fear of disapproval, fear of being misunderstood, or fear of hurting someone's feelings.

The PARQS framework offers a different way. It provides a compass to navigate these conversations not from a place of fear, but from a foundation of self-trust and integrity.

The Goal Is Integrity, Not Control

Before we break down the process, we must be clear on our purpose. When you enter a difficult conversation using your PARQS compass, the goal is not to win the argument. The goal is not to control how the other person reacts.

The goal is integrity.

Success in a difficult conversation is defined by one thing: Did you represent your own needs with clarity and kindness? If you did that, you succeeded, regardless of how they responded. You did not abandon yourself in the fire. I have found that when I release the need to manage the outcome, I am more empowered to be present with myself and my needs. This is what allows for a willingness to be open to a genuine exchange with the other person.

SCENARIO 1:

The "Holiday Dinner" Crossroads

Let's walk through a common, emotionally charged scenario. Imagine your family has an unwritten rule that everyone spends a specific holiday at your parents' house. But this year, you and your partner have a deep desire—a Preference—for a quiet, restful holiday at home. The thought of telling your parents fills you with dread.

- **Entry Point: Awareness.** Long before the conversation, you notice the dread in your body when you think about the holiday. You acknowledge the tension. This is valuable information.
- **Clarify Your Preference.** You and your partner confirm that your shared Preference is for a quiet holiday. You get clear on your "why"—it's about a need for rest and connection, not a rejection of your family.
- **Prepare with Questions.** Before speaking to your parents, you use compassionate Questions: *What is my core intention here? What is the most loving way I can express my needs?*

- **Choose the Right Action.** The Right Action is having the conversation calmly and privately. You might say something like: *"I love our family holiday traditions. This year, we've realized what we really need is some quiet time to rest at home. We won't be able to make it for the big dinner, but I would love to find another time this season for us to celebrate together."*
- **Practice Self-Acceptance.** Your parents might be understanding, or they might be disappointed. You cannot control their response. The work here is to practice Self-Acceptance. You can offer empathy (*"I understand you're disappointed"*) while holding firm to your own needs. Your success was acting with integrity.

The "Holiday Rotation" Crossroads

Now let's explore a different, equally complex holiday dynamic: the loyalty bind of being split between two or more families. The pressure to be everywhere at once can lead to a holiday season filled with frantic travel, exhaustion, and the feeling that you haven't truly been present with anyone.

- **Entry Point: Preference & Awareness.** You acknowledge your deep Preference to feel present and joyful during the holidays, not stressed and fragmented. You are Aware of the chronic anxiety this situation causes you year after year.
- **Prepare with Questions.** You shift from anxiety to strategy by asking a powerful Question: *"How can I create a fair and sustainable system that honors all of my loved ones and also protects my own well-being?"*

- **Choose the Right Action.** The Right Action is to move from a reactive, year-to-year decision to a proactive, long-term plan. You decide to institute a system of rotation. You communicate this clearly, lovingly, and well in advance of the holiday season. You might say: *"We love celebrating with all of our family, but trying to split the day has become so stressful for us. To make sure we can be fully present and enjoy our time with everyone, we've decided to start a rotation system. This year we'll be with your family for the main holiday, and next year we'll be with the other. We want to make sure the time we have together is high-quality, and this feels like the best way to do that."*

- **Practice Self-Acceptance.** There may be initial disappointment. This is where you practice Self-Acceptance. *"Of course this is a change, and it's okay for them to be disappointed. I am making a healthy, loving, and sustainable choice for myself and my relationships."* You are trading a moment of discomfort for a future of predictable structure. You are no longer deciding every year; the decision is already made.

SCENARIO 3:

The 'Pop-In' Invitation

Now let's explore a scenario that might feel familiar, especially when you are deep in a project or in need of restorative solitude. A well-meaning friend, who you genuinely like, texts you: "Hey! I'm in your neighborhood. Free for a quick coffee in 30?" Your autopilot response might be to say "yes" to be a good friend. But you are in the middle of a focused work session, finally making progress on a project that matters deeply to you. You feel torn.

- **Entry Point: Awareness & Preference.** You feel a jolt of anxiety. That's your Awareness cue. You immediately identify your Preference: you need to protect this focused time. The need is not just to work; it's to respect the commitment you've made to yourself.
- **Prepare with Questions.** You quickly move from the internal dilemma to a practical strategy by asking clarifying Questions: *How can I best communicate my needs while also letting my friend know I genuinely want to see them, just not right now? What is the clearest way to offer an alternative?*
- **Choose the Right Action.** You realize that being a good friend also means being honest. A distracted, resentful coffee is not a gift to you or to them. A clear, kind boundary is. The Right Action is a prompt, honest, and warm text message. You might write: It is so good to hear from you! I am deep in a project right now and can't break away. I would love to see you, though. Are you free next week?"
- **Practice Self-Acceptance.** Your friend might understand, or they might be disappointed. You cannot control that.

You practice Self-Acceptance by remembering that you cannot be everything to everyone at all times. You respected your need, preserved your project, and offered a genuine alternative for connection. You acted from a place of integrity.

By following this process, you transform a moment of potential conflict or self-betrayal into an act of deep self-respect.

A Moment to Check In

Bring the moment to mind. Name one conversation you have been avoiding. It might be with a colleague, a family member, or a friend.

Shift your preparation. Instead of trying to script what *they* might say, focus on what *you* need to say.

Create your anchor. Fill in the blank below. This sentence isn't for them—it's for you. *"Regardless of their reaction, the one thing I need to say to remain true to myself is..."*

Hold steady. Once you write out that sentence, you have an anchor to steady you throughout the conversation.

Reflections

The Practice of
a PARQS-Guided Life

PARQS

Chapter 11:
From Practice to Habit

You now have your compass. You have held each of the five tools—Preferences, Awareness, Right Action, Questions, and Self-Acceptance—and you have seen how they work together.

But the goal of this book is not just to give you a compass you can use in a crisis. The goal is to help you integrate it so deeply that it becomes your natural way of navigating the world.

How does this new way of being become a lasting part of your life?

Self-Trust Is Built with Evidence, Not Hope

Self-trust isn't a fixed trait you are born with. It isn't a magical insight that arrives in a flash.

Self-trust is a skill you build, brick by brick. And the mortar that holds those bricks together is **evidence**.

- Every time you pause to notice your **Preference**, you provide a piece of evidence that your needs matter.
- Every time you use **Awareness** to ground yourself, you provide evidence that you can handle the present moment.
- Every time you take a **Right Action**, no matter how small, you provide evidence that you are capable.

It is this slow, steady accumulation of evidence that rewires your brain. It builds a foundation you can stand on.

The Myth of the 21-Day Fix

In the world of self-improvement, you will often hear about the "21-day rule"—the idea that you can build a new habit in three weeks.

This sets us up for failure. When the new habit doesn't stick in three weeks, we think *we* are the problem. Research suggests that, on average, it takes 66 days for a new behavior to become automatic. For some, it takes much longer.

This is good news. It frees us from the pressure of a magical deadline. The goal isn't to be perfect for 21 days; the goal is to practice, one day at a time, for as long as it takes.

From Grand Gestures to Micro-Practices

So, how do you practice consistently without it becoming another overwhelming item on your to-do list?

Focus on micro-practices.

Instead of thinking, *"I need to master self-trust,"* think, *"Today, I will practice one minute of Awareness."*

The One-Minute PARQS Check-In

You can do this at any point in your day. It is the conscious choice to bring intention to the familiar.

- **(P)reference:** Ask yourself: *What is one thing I need or want right now?* (e.g., a glass of water, a deep breath).
- **(A)wareness:** Take one slow breath. Notice the sensation of your feet on the floor.
- **(R)ight Action:** Do the one thing you identified. Drink the water. Take the breath.

- **(Q)uestion:** Ask: *What is one kind thing I can say to myself right now?*
- **(S)elf-Acceptance:** Silently say to yourself: *I am doing the best I can in this moment.*

This is not another task to perfect. It is a moment to connect. It is one brick in your foundation.

From Concept to Lived Practice

The goal is to move the compass from a concept in your mind to a lived practice in your body.

This happens in the small, often-overlooked moments.

Here are a few ways to find your own moments of practice :

- **Your Morning Coffee:** Approach it not as a task, but as a ritual. Use it as a one-minute opportunity for **Awareness**. Notice the aroma, the warmth of the mug, and the specific taste .
- **Your Daily Commute:** Instead of seeing it as something to be endured, see it as a space for practice. At a red light, instead of reaching for your phone, take one deep breath.
- **A Repetitive Task:** Whether it is washing dishes or filing paperwork, use the rhythm of the task as an anchor.

The key is bringing fresh attention to familiar experiences . This is how you prevent your life from defaulting back to autopilot.

The Real Test: Coming Home

In my own journey, travel was the laboratory where I first forged the PARQS framework. But the real test was whether the tools still worked when I came home.

I began by testing and developing my **Preferences** at the most basic levels. I would pause and ask myself, **"What do I actually want right now?"** when making a simple choice, like deciding if I wanted water, tea, a beer, or a martini.

Then I took an extra step: I would consciously say to myself, **"I am choosing a preference."**

Over time, I noticed my internal dialogue shifted from anxiety to curiosity. I began to look forward to the pause because I knew I was taking a moment to figure out what I wanted.

There were many times I did not get an instant answer, and that was okay. The process became less about pressure and more about the act of discovery.

Through this slow, steady practice, I learned that my voice and my choices matter. I learned that I am a safe, capable provider and protector I can trust.

A Moment to Check In

Review your routine. Think about your typical day. Where is the "dead time"? (e.g., waiting for the kettle to boil, sitting in traffic, or brushing your teeth).

Plant the flag. Decide right now: *Where will I insert a One-Minute Check-In tomorrow?*

Commit to the micro. Do not promise to do it "forever." Just commit to doing it **once** tomorrow. See if you can lay just one brick.

Reflections

The PARQS Field Guide: Navigating Complex Terrain

You have the compass.

You understand the power of your **Preferences**, the clarity of **Awareness**, the integrity of **Right Action**, the compassion of **Questions**, and the courage of **Self-Acceptance**.

In this final section, we shift our focus from learning the tools to applying them in the real world.

The format of these next chapters is different. They are more direct, more practical, and designed as a hands-on field guide.

This is intentional.

Think of the first part of this book as learning to use your compass in the calm waters of a safe harbor. This final part is the open-sea voyage.

These chapters are designed as a quick reference guide. You do not need to read them in order. Return to them when you find yourself in the sticky, persistent patterns that are the most difficult to navigate.

You have the foundation. You have the compass. Now, let's continue the journey.

Chapter 12:
The Sticky Web of
a Compelling Connection

We have applied our PARQS compass to the challenges of daily life and difficult conversations. Now, we bring it to the most complex terrain of the internal world: the sticky, persistent loop of a compelling connection.

I know this pattern intimately because I have lived it.

It is a cycle that consumes immense emotional energy—especially when a part of us does not want it to end. It might be a longing for a past partner, an idealized version of a new acquaintance, or a connection that feels so profound you might use labels like "twin flame" or "mirror soul" to make sense of it.

Let me be clear: **This chapter is not here to judge the reality of your feelings.**

The deep connection you feel is real. The love is real. The significance you attribute to it is real.

However, the PARQS framework invites us to look at the *function* this loop serves in your daily life. We are looking at the patterns of longing, anxiety, and attachment so we can make choices that support your growth rather than your depletion.

A Critical Note on Safety

Before we proceed, we must make a distinction. This chapter is a guide for navigating an internal emotional pattern.

If your relationship involves fear, coercion, control, or any form of physical or emotional harm, this is not a growth exercise. It is a safety issue.

Your safety is the most critical Right Action.

Because phone numbers and organizations can change, the most reliable way to find help is to use a search engine on a **safe device** (one that the other person cannot access).

Here are effective search terms you can use to find confidential support in your area:

- *"Emotional abuse helpline [your city/state]"*
- *"Domestic violence shelter near me"*
- *"National Domestic Violence Hotline"*

Why This Loop Feels So Strong

The work of PARQS invites us to ask a courageous Question: **"Is my focus on this connection serving as an 'escape hatch' from the reality of my present moment?"**

It took me six years of persistent practice to answer "yes" to that question.

That is not a failure; that is the reality of unwinding a deep pattern. It required persistent, mostly painful practice to finally answer 'yes' to that question.

I finally saw the pattern for what it was: **A high-interest loan of emotional energy.**

We get a temporary hit of excitement or validation from the thought of this person. But the repayment terms are steep. The cost is a profound disconnection from our own lives. The problem is not the person; the problem is using the loop as a form of self-abandonment.

Navigating the Loop: A PARQS Walkthrough

Here is how to use your compass to close the escape hatch and return to yourself.

1. **Catch the loop (Awareness)** The loop is often accompanied by a rush of intense feelings—adrenaline, obsessive thoughts, or a compulsive urge to accommodate. Your first step is not to fight the feeling, but to see it .

    Micro Practice: Notice the physical sensation (e.g., racing heart, tight chest). Say to yourself: *"This feeling is the loop. It is a signal that I am avoiding something right now."* Place both feet flat on the floor for 10 seconds .

2. **Name the need (Preference)** The connection feels powerful because it is pointing to a need. Ask a compassionate Question: *"What is my focus on this person giving me that I actually need?"*

    Micro Practice: Ask: *"What feeling am I chasing right now?"* Rephrase it as a preference: *"I prefer to feel steady,"* or *"I prefer to feel energized."*

3. **Close the escape hatch (Right Action)** Every moment you spend in the loop is a moment you are not present in your own life. A powerful Right Action is to physically interrupt the mental cycle .

    Micro Practice: Choose one body-based grounding tool. Use **The 5-Sense Reset** (name 1 thing you see, 1 you hear, 1 you feel) or **The Butterfly Hug** (cross arms over chest and tap shoulders slowly for 30 seconds) .

4. **Validate the withdrawal (Self-Acceptance)** When you close the escape hatch, the feelings you were avoiding will surface. This is the moment for courageous Self-Acceptance. In my own experience, I sometimes repeated my statement ten times before I calmed down.

    Micro Practice: Take a slow inhale and a longer exhale. Place a hand on your heart. Say it aloud:
    "Of course this hurts."
    "Of course I don't want this to end."
    "Of course. Of course. Of course."

By using your compass in this way, you loosen the grip of the habit. You build the foundation of a life grounded in your own self-trust.

A Moment to Check In

Identify the loop. What is your current compelling connection or fantasy loop?

Trace the root. What unmet need is it pointing to? Is it a need for validation, excitement, or something else?

Choose the interruption. What is one small **Right Action** you can take today to meet that need in a grounded way? (e.g., calling a trusted friend instead of checking the other person's social media).

Reflections

A
R
P
PARQS
S
Q

Chapter 13:
Cultural Duty vs. Personal Dream

This chapter offers a path for when your personal dream collides with a powerful cultural or familial duty.

I know this terrain intimately. I grew up in a restrictive religious environment where my choices belonged to the community's rules.

Leaving the environment didn't erase the conditioning. For two decades, I contorted myself to keep the peace while trying to figure out how to express who I actually was.

My breakthrough came after many "re-dos" with my compass. I saw that I was seeking acceptance from a source that could not offer it in the way I needed. Step by step, I learned to provide that acceptance for myself. The grip on my heart loosened. I could end the chase.

Sometimes it feels like you can't change your external circumstances without catastrophic fallout. The cost of staying, however, is often quiet resentment.

The PARQS framework does not promise an instant escape. It offers something real: a way to reclaim internal power. It helps you move from helplessness to conscious, self-loyal choice.

A Note on Integrity & Safety

This chapter is about navigating a conflict between two positive values (e.g., your dream and your loyalty).

If your situation involves abuse, coercion, or harm, please prioritize your safety. Create distance, tell a trusted person, and seek professional support. Your well-being is the most important Right Action.

For specific search terms and resources on finding confidential support in your area, **please refer to the safety section in Chapter 12**.

- **Right Action:** If you are unsafe, do not try to "breathe through it." Prioritize your physical and emotional safety above all else. Use a safe device to search for: *"Emotional abuse helpline [your city/state]"* or *"Domestic violence shelter near me"*.

Navigating the Crossroads:
A PARQS Walkthrough

Here is how to use your compass to survive the "Either/Or" trap.

1. **Name the Suppressed Want (Preference)** Untold truth ferments into resentment. Naming your want is not rebellion; it is **data collection**.

   Micro Practice: Find a quiet moment. Take one slow inhale and a longer exhale. Say (silently or aloud): *"I would actually prefer to be [insert your real want here]."* Notice your body's response. That sensation is information, not a command .

2. **Reclaim Your Choice (Awareness)** The feeling of being "trapped" often comes from the thought, *"I have to do this."*

   Micro Practice: Catch the thought *"I can't"* or *"I'm trapped."* Reframe it to reflect your agency: *"Right now, I am **choosing** to fulfill this duty because I value [stability/family/safety]."* This restores your power as the navigator .

3. **Take a Micro-Action (Right Action)** Even if you cannot pursue your dream fully, a tiny action proves you haven't abandoned it. This is an act of Self-Loyalty.

   Micro Practice: Choose one micro-action for this week.
   Research (15 min): Read one page about your dream.
   Integrate (10 min): Sketch a logo or draft a paragraph.
   This small act keeps the pilot light of your dream alive.

4. **Reframe and Accept (Questions & Self-Acceptance)** Compassionate questions can dissolve the binary trap, and self-acceptance can soothe the parts of you that fear change.

   Micro Practice:
   Ask: *"What am I protecting by respecting this duty?"*
   Accept: Use an **Of Course** statement: *"Of course, this is hard. Of course, my dream is real. Of course, I can take one caring step for myself today."*

By using your compass in this way, you transform a situation that feels like a prison into a conscious choice. You are no longer a passenger; you are the navigator.

A Moment to Check In

Identify the conflict. Bring to mind a cultural or familial duty that feels in conflict with a personal dream.

Name the data. What is one "Micro-Preference" you could name for yourself today, even if you cannot act on it yet?

Reflections

A
R
P
S
Q
PARQS

Chapter 14:
The Caregiver's Compass:
Navigating Duty and Devotion

We now bring our PARQS compass to a situation that many of us will face in our lives, one that sits at the complex intersection of love, duty, and self-preservation: the role of the family caregiver.

This is not a theoretical problem; it is a lived reality of immense emotional and physical weight.

The duty of caring for a loved one—a parent, a partner, a child—is a high and noble value. But when that devotion leads to a state of chronic exhaustion, it can feel like a crushing, unsustainable dilemma.

The conflict is often between your deep sense of responsibility for another and the non-negotiable need to care for yourself.

In these moments, the PARQS framework is not a tool for escaping your duty. It is a compass for navigating this challenge in a way that is sustainable, self-loyal, and ultimately more loving for everyone involved.

A Note on Seeking Support

The work of a caregiver is demanding. The tools in this chapter are designed to help you reclaim your internal agency and prevent burnout.

They are not a substitute for seeking and accepting practical support.

Whether from other family members, community resources, or professional agencies, asking for help is a powerful **Right Action**.

The Caregiver's Compass: A PARQS Walkthrough

Here is how to use your compass to find sustainability within the duty.

1. **Acknowledge the Reality (Awareness).** An honest step is to anchor in the reality of your body. Your body is the most honest accountant of your energy. The chronic fatigue, the tension in your shoulders, the quiet resentment that simmers under the surface—these are not signs of weakness. They are your Awareness cues.

   Micro Practice (60 Seconds): Close your eyes for a moment. Scan your body from head to toe. Where are you holding the most tension right now? Say to yourself: *"This feeling of exhaustion is real information. My body is telling me something needs to change."*

2. **Name the Unspoken Need (Preference)** In the caregiver role, it is easy to silence your own needs. The practice here is to give yourself permission to name the human Preference you have been pushing aside. This is not selfish; it is essential.

   Micro Practice (60 Seconds): Ask yourself: *"If I could have one small thing for myself right now, what would it be?"* Name the preference, no matter how "unrealistic" it may seem: *"I prefer to have two hours completely to myself this week."*

3. **Move to Problem-Solving (Questions)** Once you have named your preference, you can shift from a state of overwhelm to one of practical problem-solving.

   Micro Practice (60 Seconds): Ask a solution-focused question: *"How can I respect my obligation, while also taking the smallest possible step toward getting two hours of rest?"* or *"Who is one person I could ask for a small amount of help?"*

4. **Take a Self-Loyal Action (Right Action)** A courageous Right Action for a caregiver is often to ask for help or to create a clear, kind boundary. This is not an act of abandonment; it is an act of necessary self-preservation.

   Micro Practice (90 Seconds): Identify one person or resource you could reach out to this week. Script your request: *"I need help covering a two-hour window every Tuesday, or I will not be able to continue at this pace."*

5. **Soothe the Guilt (Self-Acceptance)** The moment you ask for help or set a boundary, the feeling of guilt will almost certainly arise. This is the moment for courageous Self-Acceptance.

> **Micro Practice (60 Seconds):** Use an **Of Course** sequence to meet the guilt with compassion:
> *"Of course, I feel guilty asking for help."*
> *"Of course, I'm used to being the one who handles everything."*
> *"Of course, I am choosing to respect my own limits so I can be present for the long run."*

By using your compass in this way, you are not choosing *between* your duty and yourself. You are finding a way to honor both.

A Moment to Check In

Scan for truth. If you are in a caregiver role, take a moment to notice your body. What is the primary feeling you notice right now?

Name the need. What is one small **Preference** you have been silencing?

Validate the struggle. Fill in the blank: *"Of course I am tired, because..."*

Anchor yourself. Remind yourself that your well-being is the engine that allows you to care for others. Protecting the engine is not selfish; it is required.

Reflections

A
R
P
S
Q
PARQS

Chapter 15:
Navigating Imposter Syndrome

We now bring our compass to one of the most persistent and isolating internal patterns: the feeling of being a fraud.

Imposter syndrome is the heavy feeling that your accomplishments are a fluke, that you do not deserve your success, and that you will eventually be "found out".

I know this terrain well. For a long time, despite external evidence of my competence, I lived with a quiet, internal dread that I didn't truly belong.

I didn't know the label "imposter syndrome" existed, yet I lived with all its symptoms. I would complete a project and give the accomplishment very little notice. But the moment someone else acknowledged what I had done, my system turned erratic.

Receiving a direct compliment felt physically challenging. I was confidently doing my work, but living in fear that I was about to get the boot.

It took me fifteen years of persistent practice—countless re-dos with my PARQS compass—to loosen the grip of this pattern.

The most powerful **Right Action** was learning to build my own internal case file of evidence, separate from anyone else's validation.

Today, I can receive a compliment for what it is: another person's genuine gratitude. It is an incredible experience to hear a kind word, say "thank you," and feel calm inside. That peace is not something that happened to me; it is something I built.

This feeling is not a sign of inadequacy; ironically, it is most common among high achievers. It is a story your Inner Critic tells you.

The PARQS compass is a practical tool to navigate this, not by trying to argue with the feeling, but by systematically building a case file of evidence for your own capability.

Navigating the Feeling:
A PARQS Walkthrough

Here is how to move from feeling like a fraud to trusting your track record.

1. **1. Name the Story (Awareness)** The first step is to recognize the feeling when it arises. The racing heart before a presentation, the urge to downplay a success, the thought *"I have no idea what I'm doing"*—these are your Awareness cues.

   Micro Practice (60 Seconds): When the feeling hits, pause. Notice the physical sensation (e.g., tight chest). Label the experience silently: *"This is the imposter story. It feels real, but it is a familiar pattern of thought."*

2. **State Your Preference (Preference).** Underneath the fear of being a fraud is a desire to feel capable. Your Preference is to stand in the truth of your efforts.

   Micro Practice (60 Seconds): Ask: *"What would I actually prefer to feel right now?"* State it clearly: *"I prefer to acknowledge my hard work,"* or *"I prefer to trust in my preparation."*

3. **Build Your Evidence Log (Right Action)** Imposter syndrome thrives on a lack of concrete, accessible evidence. Your most powerful Right Action is to create that evidence for yourself.

   Micro Practice (90 Seconds): Open a new note on your phone. Title it **"My Evidence Log."** Write down one specific accomplishment from the last month, one piece of positive feedback you received, or one skill you possess. The next time the "imposter story" starts, your Right Action is to read this log.

4. **Reframe the Question (Questions)** The imposter story is fueled by fearful questions like, *"What if they find out I'm a fraud?"*

   Micro Practice (60 Seconds): Catch the fearful question. Replace it with an evidence-based one: *"What is one piece of objective evidence that I am prepared for this?"* or *"What would I tell a respected friend if they were feeling this way?"*

5. **Validate the Feeling, Not the Story (Self-Acceptance)**
    The anxiety is real, even if the story causing it is not.
    The final step is to offer yourself Self-Acceptance for the
    discomfort of the experience.

    Micro Practice (60 Seconds): Use a specific **Of
    Course** statement: *"Of course I am feeling anxious;
    this is important to me, and I want to do well."*

A Moment to Check In

Identify the trigger. In what specific situations does your "imposter story" tend to get the loudest? (e.g., starting a new project, receiving a compliment) .

Gather the proof. What is one piece of evidence you can add to your "Evidence Log" right now?

Anchor the truth. Write it down. Do not dismiss it as "luck" or "timing." Own it as a fact.

Reflections

Chapter 16:
Navigating a Career Change

A career change is one of the most significant navigational challenges we can face. It sits at the intersection of our identity, our security, and our future goals.

The process often feels like a fog of endless options, clouded by external expectations and the loud voice of the Inner Critic telling you it's too late, too risky, or that you're not qualified.

I can relate to that feeling deeply.

In my own experience, a major career shift felt less like an exciting opportunity and more like a personal failing. Growing up, the message I absorbed was that not "working" in a traditional sense equaled being lazy.

So when my last enterprise ended unexpectedly, I went into a tailspin. I had been so focused on the work that I never thought of a Plan B. I had no idea what my next direction would be.

What followed was a year and a half in the "messy middle." The uncertainty was a constant companion.

However, by consistently using my PARQS compass, I was able to navigate those peaks and valleys.

- **Awareness:** When the feeling of being a victim arose, I noticed it.
- **Self-Acceptance:** I used a powerful **Of Course** statement: *"Of course I'm feeling lost right now; my entire professional identity just ended abruptly."*

This practice created the space for a new realization to emerge. I began to understand that the personal development work I had done over the past thirty years had immense value. Once I came to that realization, my next **Right Action** became clear: to share the framework that had helped me.

The pressure to make the one "perfect" choice leads to paralysis. The PARQS compass offers a different approach. It guides you to navigate this change not by trying to find the perfect answer "out there," but by building clarity from the inside, one small, intentional step at a time.

Navigating the Crossroads:
A PARQS Walkthrough

Here is how to turn a career crisis into a series of manageable experiments.

1. **Dial Down the Noise (Awareness & Preference)** Before you open a single job board, the first step is to get quiet. A career change is often clouded by a chorus of "shoulds".

   Micro Practice (90 Seconds): Find a quiet space and close your eyes. Ask yourself: *"Putting aside salary, titles, and what anyone else would think, what is one thing I want to feel in my workday?"* Is it creativity? Calm? A sense of purpose? Connection? That feeling is your first navigational star.

2. **Run a Small Experiment (Right Action)** Clarity comes from action, not from thought alone. The most powerful Right Action you can take is a small, low-stakes experiment to gather real-world data.

    Micro Practice (90 Seconds): Based on the feeling you identified, brainstorm one tiny experiment.
    - If you want to feel "creative," sign up for a 30-minute online tutorial.
    - If you want "connection," reach out to one person on LinkedIn for a 15-minute virtual coffee.
    - Do not commit to a career path. Commit to a 15-minute experiment.

3. **Ask Generative Questions (Questions)** Analysis paralysis is fueled by dead-end questions like, *"What is the perfect job for me?"*

    Micro Practice (60 Seconds): Catch the overwhelming question. Replace it with a generative one: *"What am I curious to learn more about?"* or *"What is one small step that feels interesting right now?"*

4. **Accept the Messy Middle (Self-Acceptance)** A career change is not a clean, linear path. It is a "messy middle" filled with uncertainty and "re-dos." Resisting these feelings keeps you stuck longer.

   Micro Practice (60 Seconds): When you feel discouraged, place a hand on your heart. Use a specific **Of Course** statement: *"Of course I am feeling scared and confused; this is a big transition and the path isn't clear yet. I am navigating the best I can."*

A Moment to Check In

Name the pressure. Identify one "should" (from your family, society, or yourself) that is making your career navigation feel heavier than it needs to be.

Design a micro-experiment. What is the smallest, least intimidating experiment you could run in the next seven days to gather more information?

Focus on the feedback. Do not worry about the outcome. Your only job is to run the experiment and see how it feels. That feeling is the **information** you need.

Reflections

Conclusion:
The Foundation You Can Stand On

We began this journey together by giving a name to a heavy, unnamed feeling: the feeling of living on "Remote Control."

It was the sense of being a passenger in your own life, moving through the days on autopilot, guided by a quiet chorus of "shoulds".

Look at how far you have come.

You have learned that the way out of that state is not about becoming someone new. It is about returning to who you have been all along.

You have been given a compass—a practical, down-to-earth set of tools to navigate your way back to yourself.

You now have a framework for listening to your **Preferences**, cultivating **Awareness**, taking **Right Action**, asking compassionate **Questions**, and offering yourself the profound gift of **Self-Acceptance**.

This is the work. This is **a way** to build a foundation of deep self-trust, brick by brick.

For me, the starting point was the frustration of "not being able to name the roots of my problems". Through **developing and practicing** this framework, I was able to chip away at that stuckness.

I am now empowered to choose, pivot, and trust myself as safe and capable.

This is my story, **and** the purpose of sharing it has always been to show you what is possible for your own **story**.

Your time of being lost to "Remote Control Living" is **one brick closer to being** over. You have the compass.

The lifelong, rewarding journey of using it has just begun.

Welcome home to yourself.

Appendix A:
A Toolkit for Your PARQS Practice

This section contains a small collection of powerful, practical tools that you can use to support your PARQS practice. Think of these as micro-practices designed to help you in moments of overwhelm, anxiety, or disconnection. Each one takes only a minute or two and can be done anywhere.

A Grounding Exercise
using Your Five Senses

What it is: An exercise to ground you in your physical surroundings by methodically naming things you can perceive with your five senses. **How it supports your PARQS practice:** This is a primary tool for activating your Awareness. It pulls your focus out of the noise of your mind (the Inner Critic, worries about the future) and anchors you in the present moment, calming your nervous system.

How to do it:

- Name **5** things you can see around you.
- Name **4** things you can feel.
- Name **3** things you can hear.
- Name **2** things you can smell.
- Name **1** thing you can taste.

Box Breathing

What it is: A simple, rhythmic breathing technique used to calm the body and focus the mind. **How it supports your PARQS practice:** This is a powerful Right Action you can take when you feel overwhelmed. It directly regulates your nervous system, creating the internal space needed for Awareness and compassionate Questions to arise.

How to do it:

- Breathe in slowly through your nose for 4 counts.
- Hold your breath for 4 counts.
- Breathe out slowly through your mouth for 4 counts.
- Hold the empty breath for 4 counts.
- Repeat the cycle for one to two minutes, or until you feel a sense of calm.

The Butterfly Hug

What it is: A self-soothing technique that uses bilateral stimulation (tapping both sides of the body) to create a sense of safety and calm. How it supports your PARQS practice: This is a tangible act of Self-Acceptance and Self-Loyalty. In moments when you feel overwhelmed or are struggling with your Inner Critic, it is a physical way of being on your own side and offering yourself comfort.

How to do it:

- Cross your arms over your chest, with your right hand on your left shoulder and your left hand on your right shoulder. Your hands and arms will look like the wings of a butterfly.
- Begin to gently and slowly tap your shoulders, alternating between your left and right hand.
- Breathe slowly and deeply as you continue to tap for one to two minutes. This practice can be especially helpful after using an "Of Course" Statement, as it provides a physical reinforcement of your self-acceptance.

Appendix B:
Frequently Asked Questions &
Deeper Dives

This section is for those moments when you hit a roadblock, when the practice feels difficult, or when you are ready to explore the deeper principles of this work. These are answers to the questions that naturally arise when you begin the important journey of building your own internal guidance system.

Q: I've been trying to use the PARQS compass, but I feel like it's not working. What am I doing wrong?

First, let's approach this with a compassionate Question instead of a judgment: *What does "not working" feel like?* Often, when we say something "isn't working," we mean, "I'm not getting the result I wanted" or "This still feels uncomfortable." This is a critical moment in your practice, and it is not a sign of failure. It is an invitation to go deeper. This brings us to a core principle of this work: Radical Self-Responsibility. This is the commitment to be an active participant in your own growth, knowing that every moment of practice is another brick being laid in your foundation.

Q: I've tried pausing to ask, *'actually*, what do I want?', but I cannot find my preference. My mind just goes blank.

This is an honest and important observation. First, know that your mind is not "broken"—it's operating on a well-trained autopilot. For years, you likely taught your mind to silence your inner voice to prioritize the needs of others. Your "Preference" muscle has simply atrophied from lack of use. The feeling of going blank is not a failure; it is your Awareness cue that the foundation of your self-trust is still being built. Here's how to use your compass to navigate the silence: get out of your head and into your body. Use a micro-practice like the grounding exercise using your five senses. Then, ask an easier question: *"What am I actively trying to avoid right now?"* It is often easier to name a rejection than it is to name a desire.

Q: I don't feel anything. How can I notice where the physical sensation is?

If you feel numb or disconnected, it's likely your mind developed an effective strategy to dampen emotional signals. The absence of feeling is also a form of Awareness itself. Here is how to practice when you feel nothing at all: instead of asking, "What emotion am I feeling?" ask, "What is currently physically unavoidable?" Anchor yourself to constants that have no emotional charge: the weight of your feet on the floor, the sound of your own breath, the points of contact between your body and the chair.

Q: I feel impatient with my progress. Why do I keep getting stuck on the same lessons?

In my own journey, I discovered that by disrespecting my current place on the learning curve, I was short-changing myself of the very skills I needed for the future. The more I rushed, the longer the lesson seemed to last. When you notice a thought like, "I should be better at this by now," try adding one word: *"I'm not better at this yet."* Honoring your current stage is a powerful way to accelerate your progress.

Q: I've started setting boundaries and prioritizing my needs, but now I feel guilty. Is that normal?

Yes, it is completely normal. For many of us, guilt is the first and most powerful form of resistance we encounter when we step off autopilot. For years, your nervous system was trained to believe that "keeping others happy = safety." When you choose your own needs, your brain can initially interpret this as a threat, and it sends out guilt as a warning signal to get you back in line. The work is not to avoid guilt, but to learn to see it for what it is. Use your compass: notice the guilt in your body (Awareness), ask what it's trying to protect you from (Question), and meet it with an "Of Course" statement (Self-Acceptance): *"Of course I feel guilty. I am learning a new way of being, and it feels unfamiliar. This feeling is a sign that I am growing."*

Q: I've been using the PARQS compass to set boundaries, but it's causing friction with people in my life. Did I do something wrong?

Absolutely not. In fact, this is often a sign that you are doing the work correctly. For years, your relationships have operated on a set of unwritten rules based on your old patterns. When you begin to change those patterns, you are changing the rules of engagement. It is natural for the people around you to react to it. This is not a sign of your failure, but evidence of your growth. The work here is not to manage their reaction, but to manage your own. This is an important opportunity to practice Self-Loyalty. You are not responsible for other people's feelings, but you are responsible for representing your own needs with integrity.

Appendix C:
PARQS Framework Glossary

This glossary provides a quick reference for the core concepts and tools of the PARQS framework. These are not academic definitions, but practical, down-to-earth explanations to support your journey.

Autopilot (or "Remote Control Living") What it is: A state of moving through life guided by habit, routine, and the expectations of others, rather than by your own conscious choices. **Think of it as:** Being a passenger in the car of your own life.

The Inner Critic What it is: The voice in your head that judges, doubts, and criticizes you. It is the internal echo of past conditioning and fears. **Think of it as:** A well-intentioned but misguided security guard, trying to keep you "safe" by keeping you small.

OF COURSE (The Acronym) What it is: A powerful declaration of Self-Loyalty embedded in the "Of Course" Statement, serving as your internal cheer team. **What it stands for:** Open • Fearless • Cogent • Overcoming • Unrelenting • Resolved • Systematic • Evolving. **Think of it as:** The support crew you activate with a single phrase.

PARQS Compass What it is: The complete, five-part internal guidance system (Preferences, Awareness, Right Action, Questions, Self-Acceptance). **Think of it as:** A multi-tool, like a Swiss Army Knife, where any one tool can be your entry point to access the others.

Radical Self-Responsibility What it is: The commitment to take 100% ownership of your practice and your responses, without blame. **Think of it as:** Realizing you are not just a character in your own story, but also the author.

Self-Acceptance & Self-Loyalty What they are: Self-Acceptance is the in-the-moment practice of validating your feelings without judgment. Self-Loyalty is the underlying principle of not abandoning your own needs. **Think of it as:** Self-Loyalty is the commitment to be on your own team. Self-Acceptance is how you act as a good teammate in a difficult moment.

"Trust Your Gut" (The PARQS Definition) What it is: The destination, not the starting point. It is the intuitive knowing that arises after you have consistently built self-trust through evidence. **Think of it as:** The effortless performance that comes after many hours of deliberate practice.

"Moving Forward" (The Mindset) What it is: A conscious declaration to shift your focus from a past mistake to the next possible Right Action. **Think of it as:** The moment you turn the car around after a wrong turn, focusing on the road ahead instead of the mistake.

"Yet" (The Word as a Tool) What it is: A single word that transforms a statement of fixed identity into a statement of progress. **Think of it as:** A bridge from a closed-door statement to an open-path possibility (e.g., "I'm not good at this... yet.").

Appendix D:
Sources and Inspirations for the Practices

This book is built on a foundation of my own lived experience, but it is also deeply informed and inspired by the work of many brilliant teachers, researchers, and practitioners. This section serves to honor their contributions and provide a path for you to explore their work more deeply.

Pausing to Ask "Actually, What Do I Want? (Chapter 2) The principle of creating a deliberate "pause" between a trigger and a response is a cornerstone of many respected mindfulness and therapeutic traditions. I am grateful for the foundational work in this area, including the "STOP" skill in Dialectical Behavior Therapy (DBT), Tara Brach's "RAIN" meditation, and the cognitive defusion techniques of Acceptance and Commitment Therapy (ACT). My specific application of this 'pause' is as a radically simple, language-based tool with one specific purpose: to begin the practice of identifying your Preferences. While other protocols are often focused on emotional regulation or defusing from thoughts, this pause-and-ask method is a radically simple, language-based tool with one specific purpose: to begin the practice of identifying your Preferences. It is a micro-tool designed to create the initial space needed to ask, "What do I actually want?".

A Grounding Exercise Using Your Five Senses (Chapter 3 & Appendix A). This widely used grounding exercise is often referred to as the '5,4,3,2,1 Technique.' We are grateful to the pioneers in this field, such as Betty Alice Erickson, who was instrumental in developing and popularizing its use as a therapeutic tool.

The Power of Questions (**Chapter 5**) My understanding of the power of reframing and asking compassionate questions has been profoundly shaped by my work with my therapist, Jennifer S. Baily, M.A., LMFT, who first asked me the pivotal question, "What does Elaina want?".

Right Action & Saying "No" (**Chapter 4**) My ability to take Right Action, especially the difficult act of saying "no," was greatly influenced by the work of Byron Katie. Her books, particularly *I Need Your Love – Is That True?* and *Loving What Is*, provided invaluable lessons on questioning the stories that keep us stuck.

Permission for Physical Release (**Chapter 6** & Appendix A) The concept of safely discharging emotional energy has deep roots in somatic therapy. The work of pioneers like Peter A. Levine, Ph.D., has been influential in understanding how the body can release stress. The specific practice of clenching and releasing muscles described in this book is inspired by the well-researched Progressive Muscle Relaxation, developed by Dr. Edmund Jacobson.

The "Of Course" Statement (**Chapter 6**). This powerful tool for self-acceptance was adapted from a technique I learned from Dr. Linda Howe in her work, *Healing Through the Akashic Records*.

The "OF COURSE" Acronym (**Chapter 6**) This is a personal framework I developed as my own practice deepened, allowing me to unpack the layers of Self-Loyalty contained within the "Of Course" Statement.

Uncovering Unmet Needs (Appendix B) The powerful question, "What need am I trying to have met right now?", is inspired by the foundational work of Dr. Marshall B. Rosenberg, PhD, the creator of Nonviolent Communication (NVC). His teaching on identifying the universal human needs that drive our feelings and actions is a cornerstone of compassionate self-inquiry.

Values and Perspective (Chapters 5 & 9) The work of Dr. John F. Demartini, particularly his Breakthrough Experience® program, was instrumental in teaching me how to shift perspectives and identify my own core values. This understanding is foundational to choosing a Right Action and living in a way that is truly supportive of yourself.

Appendix E:
Prompts for Your PARQS Practice

This appendix offers a set of invitations to deepen your PARQS practice. Think of this not as homework, but as a space for curiosity. The goal is to begin the "brick by brick" process of generating real-world evidence that you can trust yourself. There are no right or wrong answers; there is only the practice of noticing. Return to these prompts whenever you feel stuck or wish to reconnect with your internal compass.

Prompts for Preference
(Self-Honesty)

Recall the story of the therapist's question, "What does Elaina want?". Think of an area in your life (work, family, social commitments) where, if you were asked what you want, your mind might go blank. What does that feeling of "blankness" feel like in your body?

Prompts for Awareness
(Self-Regulation)

Think of a routine task you do on autopilot, like your daily commute or washing the dishes. The next time you do it, set an intention to notice three sensory details you normally miss. What does the water feel like? What specific sounds can you hear outside your car?

Prompts for Right Action
(Self-Integrity)

Reflect on my story of changing my mind in Malaysia. Is there a "yes" you have given recently that now feels out of alignment with your needs? What is one small, courageous step you could take to honor your new preference, even if it feels uncomfortable?

Integrity is built through evidence. What is the smallest possible action you could take today that would serve as one "brick" in your foundation of self-trust? (e.g., drinking a glass of water when you're thirsty, stretching for two minutes, saying no to a small, additional request) .

Prompts for Questions
(Self-Compassion)

Recall the last time you felt "stuck" or made a mistake. What was the judgmental, dead-end question your Inner Critic asked? (e.g., "Why can't I get this right?", "What's wrong with me?") .

Now, practice the skill of Self-Compassion. Re-write that accusatory question into a compassionate, curious one that starts with "What" or "How" (e.g., "What can I learn from this?" or "What support do I need right now?").

Prompts for Self-Acceptance
(Self-Loyalty)

If you have started setting new boundaries and are feeling the sting of guilt, see it as a sign of growth. Offer yourself this validation: "Of course I feel guilty. I am unlearning a lifetime of putting others first, and this is a new and unfamiliar feeling. This feeling is evidence that I am growing".

Consider the practice of safe physical release. What is one small, private way you could discharge physical energy when you feel overwhelmed? (e.g., pressing your feet firmly into the floor, a deep sigh, clenching and releasing your fists).

Deepening Your "Of Course" Practice

The "Of Course" Statement is your primary tool for in-the-moment Self-Loyalty. Use these prompts to move from simply saying the words to fully embodying their power.

- **Make It Specific:** Think of a mild frustration you are feeling right now. Instead of a general statement, make it highly detailed. For example, instead of "Of course I'm stressed," try "Of course I'm feeling tension in my shoulders; I have a deadline and the phone has been ringing all morning". Notice if the added detail makes the feeling of acceptance stronger.

- **Target the Inner Critic:** The next time you hear your Inner Critic's voice ("You're not doing enough," "You messed that up"), meet it directly with an "Of Course" statement. "Of course, my Inner Critic is loud right now; I'm trying something new and it's trying to keep me safe". This validates the fear without validating the criticism.

- **Embody the Acronym:** Look back at the "OF COURSE" acronym in Chapter 6. Which of those words—Open • Fearless • Cogent • Overcoming • Unrelenting • Resolved • Systematic • Evolving—do you need to connect with the most right now? Craft an "Of course" statement that specifically invokes that quality. For example: "Of course, this feels hard, and I am choosing to be Unrelenting in my commitment to myself through this moment".

This collection of prompts is just a starting point. If you found this guided practice helpful and are looking for a more comprehensive, structured journey to integrate these tools into your daily life, you may be interested in the companion PARQS Framework Workbook.

Acknowledgements

I am thankful for all the teachers and supportive individuals who have seen me, guided me, and continue to support me as I learn to live my PARQS—to ask questions, develop preferences, become aware, take the right action, and learn how to develop self-acceptance.

I am grateful to myself for my resilience, persistence, courage, and my PARQS compass.

To my mother. To say our relationship has been complex would be putting it mildly. Through my own persistence and growth, I have come to a place of greater understanding and peace. For decades, I tried to save her because she asked, and I thought it was my job. Growing up, I served the role of the "fixer," a self-abandoning pattern I had to unlearn. My journey involved years of applying my PARQS compass to our dynamic. I had to use Awareness to see the pattern clearly and compassionate Questions to understand my part in it. My breakthrough finally came when I took the Right Action of putting my own dictionary down—the one where I was trying to define her through my own terms and what I needed her to be for me. Through this, I grew to a place where I could finally hear her, appreciate her unique point of view, and practice Self-Acceptance by holding space for her. Most importantly, I learned to provide that love, validation, and protection for myself, which has empowered me to trust myself as safe and capable. It has taken thirty years to understand and integrate this. I can now say with clarity and peace that she loves me, wants the best for me, and always wishes me well.

To Sydney, my mentor, guardian, and dearest friend. From the moment we met, you have been a source of unwavering support, seeing me and loving me unconditionally. Through thirty years of peaks, valleys, and countless re-dos, you have always been available, showing me by your example that unconditional love exists. I am forever grateful. Thank you.

To Joseph, whose persistent encouragement first led me to travel the world and, in doing so, to find my own independence. Though our path has changed, his role as a mentor, champion, and best friend has never wavered. For thirty years, he has been a source of unconditional love and steadfast belief in me. His unwavering friendship is one of the greatest gifts of my life, and for it, I am deeply grateful. Thank you.

To the many teachers, specialists, and therapists who shaped my path, I offer deep gratitude. Especially to my therapist, Jennifer S. Baily, M.A., LMFT, who has supported and continues to help me find answers within myself. My gratitude to Byron Katie, whose work taught me invaluable lessons, including how to say "no." My thanks to Dr. Robert Dee McDonald, who taught me how to ask questions that shifted me from reactive answers to deep introspection. Thank you to Ines Simpson for teaching me how to connect deeply with my unconscious mind. Thank you to Robert Gene Smith, who taught me how to change emotions associated with traumatic memories, and to Dr. Sue Morter, who taught me the power of my breath. My deep appreciation to Dr. John F. Demartini, whose work taught me to change perspectives and find my core values. Thank you.

About the Author

Elaina Kelly Smith's life has been less of a gentle journey and more of an emotionally action-packed odyssey. Her path wasn't always sunlit; often, it was simply about putting one foot in front of the other, weighed down by a sense of disconnection she couldn't name.

Coming from a highly restrictive upbringing, Elaina never imagined a life of global travel. Yet, an unexpected friendship opened the world to her, and she began a series of adventures that would take her to all seven continents. It was during her courageous solo travels that she built the foundation of her self-reliance. Navigating foreign places, cultures, and situations on her own taught her something she'd never had before: trust in her ability to figure things out as she went.

These travels became her laboratory for personal growth. Despite building successful businesses, she found that external achievements couldn't solve the internal feeling of being on "autopilot." Her journey of self-discovery, which included years of spiritual searching and deep therapeutic work, was a persistent, **step by step** process of chipping away at the mistaken beliefs that were holding her back.

This persistent exploration—both external and internal—led her to develop the PARQS framework, the practical, down-to-earth compass for building self-trust that is at the heart of this book. It was through this work that she found her way out of "remote control" living into a more intentional and present existence. Her pivotal realization, prompted by her therapist's simple question,

"What does Elaina want?", empowered her to create the very system she now shares with her readers.

For Elaina, the ultimate expression of this work is in service to others. Her philanthropic efforts are a natural extension of the PARQS principles—using Awareness to see a need and taking Right Action to meet it. Whether traversing mountainous roads to reach fourteen isolated centers for visually impaired children across Vietnam, working with at-risk youth in the Philippines, or spearheading the installation of twenty-five water pumps and personally delivering food and school supplies to rural families in Cambodia, her focus is on direct, practical impact. She believes that the journey of returning to oneself is what gives us the capacity to show up for ourselves and the world with clarity and purpose.

Index

E

escape hatch — 88, 89, 90
Evidence — 77, 113, 115

F

Field Guide — 85
From Practice to Habit — 77

G

Guilt — 106

H

Holiday Dinner — 66

I

Imposter Syndrome — 111
Inner Critic — 5, 31, 33, 39, 50, 112, 119, 129, 131, 137, 145, 146

J

Jennifer S. Baily — 140, 148

M

Malaysia — 26, 144
messy middle — 119, 122
Micro-Practices — 78

N

Note on Safety — 88

O

Of Course — 38, 39, 59, 97, 106, 114, 120, 122, 131, 135, 137, 140, 146

P

Q

R

S

Did This Book Help You Find Clarity?

Thank you for completing this journey. If this book helped you find even a moment of clarity, please help the next person start their own journey to self-trust by leaving an honest review on Amazon or Goodreads. Your story matters.

Ready to Go Deeper?

This book is the "why-to" and "what-to." The upcoming 5-week course is the "how-to" system.

If you are ready to turn the PARQS Method into a practical, daily system for building deep self-trust, join the official waitlist.

The Changing Course Gracefully 5-Week Course. Be the first to know when enrollment opens. **Visit: elainakellysmith.com/course**

More from the *Changing Course Gracefully* Ecosystem

Book 2 (Workbook) *The Changing Course Gracefully Workbook: A 5-Step Guide to Build a Foundation of Deep Self-Trust*

Book 3 (Travel Journal) *Changing Course Gracefully: A Travel Journal: A Guided Travel Journal for Calm, Clarity, and Self-Trust*

Book 4 (Memoir) *An Emotionally Action-Packed Odyssey: My Journey to Find a Graceful Path*

About Ventures & Bloom Press

Ventures & Bloom Press is an independent publisher dedicated to providing practical, "down-to-earth" tools for personal growth. Our mission is to publish clear, actionable, and authentic guides for successful people who feel disconnected or stuck on "autopilot".

Our publishing philosophy is "invitational," not "prescriptive". We focus on providing tangible, "brick-by-brick" frameworks that empower readers to build foundational self-trust. We are dedicated to the real, practical steps of the journey, helping readers navigate their lives with clarity and purpose.

www.ingramcontent.com/pod-product-compliance
Lightning Source LLC
Chambersburg PA
CBHW020541160726
47991CB00002B/529